Half Yard
Heaven

Easy sewing projects using
left-over pieces of fabric

Debbie Shore

SEARCH PRESS

First published in Great Britain 2014

Search Press Limited
Wellwood, North Farm Road,
Tunbridge Wells, Kent TN2 3DR

Reprinted 2014

Photographs by Garie Hind
Styling by Kimberley Hind

ISBN: 978-1-84448-892-6

Suppliers
For details of suppliers, please visit the Search
Press website: www.searchpress.com.

Printed in China

Acknowledgements

This one is for my wonderful
photographer husband who puts up
with the constant hum of my sewing
machine, trips over the endless rolls of
fabric and picks up the loose threads
that follow me everywhere. Who
barely sees me when I'm in sewing
mode, unless to surface excitedly after
finishing a project demanding it be
photographed NOW! And still creates
the most beautiful pictures you see in
this book, and loves me despite my
having a head full of notions.

Thank you also to Kimberley Hind,
Elise and Sadie Collie for modelling my
pieces so beautifully.

Contents

Book Bag,
page 16

Wet-wipe Sachet Cover,
page 20

Tote Bag,
page 22

Glasses Case,
page 42

Craft Caddy,
page 46

Neck Cushion,
page 50

Oven Gloves,
page 68

Notice Board,
page 70

Pincushion,
page 74

Slippers,
page 76

Coat-hanger Tidy,
page 80

Make-up Bag,
page 26

Child's Apron,
page 28

Make-up Brush Roll,
page 32

Peg Bag,
page 36

Pocket Apron,
page 38

Owl and Pussy Cat,
page 52

Chicken Doorstop,
page 56

Padded Coat Hanger,
page 60

Rosette Headband,
page 62

Place Mat,
page 66

Pan Holder,
page 82

Tea Cosy,
page 84

Sewing Machine Dust
Cover, page 86

String of Hearts,
page 90

Tissue Box Cover,
page 92

Introduction

Have you ever wondered what to do with all those off-cuts and leftover pieces of fabric after you've finished a sewing project? Maybe you've bought some pretty fat quarters but don't know what to do with them. It feels wasteful to throw them away, but they aren't quite big enough to make anything useful – or so you think. Here are some quick and easy projects that are kind to your pocket and to the environment, all designed to be made with pieces of fabric less than half a yard long.

Woven fabrics like cotton or polycotton mixes work best with these projects, but don't forget to recycle … the fabric could equally as well come from an old shirt, duvet cover or tablecloth as from a fabric store! And don't forget to put your own spin on things. There's no reason why you couldn't apply a flower or rosette to your tote bag, buttons to your headband or cross-stitch to your craft caddy!

Hand-sewn items are expensive to buy, but we often lack the confidence to try making them ourselves. All the projects in this book are designed to be easy to make, even if you are a complete beginner, and can be created in just a few hours for very little money.

Be inspired, get creative, and you will soon be making beautiful, hand-made gifts that your family and friends will treasure. And if you can't bear to part with them they will add a real designer touch to your home.

Useful things

Sewing machine: a basic machine is fine as a straight stitch is really all you need for most of the projects in this book. Embroidery stitches are good for adding decoration, and zigzag stitch is great for stopping seams from fraying.

Fabric: lots of it! Sewing is an addictive hobby and it's good to have a large stash at hand. I've used cotton and polycotton mixes in this book, but feel free to experiment with other materials. Oilcloth is great for kitchen projects as it is waterproof and wipeable. Save leftover pieces from larger sewing projects, and rummage through the oddments box in your local fabric store. Keep old clothes, sheets and duvet covers – often the fabric is fine even when the item itself is no longer wanted.

Threads: a box full of coordinating and contrasting threads is always useful. Don't be tempted to buy cheap ones – the better the quality of thread you use, the better the quality of the stitching.

Buttons: collect all sorts of buttons to decorate your projects – plastic, colourful, metal, you can never have enough!

Ribbon: a ribbon makes a lovely decorative finish.

Bias-binding tape: I use this in many of the projects to give a neat and contrasting edge to an item.

Zips: remove zips from old clothes before you throw them away and keep a few in your sewing box – you never know when you'll need one.

Scissors: sharp dressmaker's shears that you use only with fabrics are a must-have in your sewing box for precision cutting. Small, sharp scissors are useful for snipping threads.

Pinking shears: these help to stop your fabric fraying, but also give a decorative edge.

Pins: I use pins with big glass heads as they are easier to see.

Steam iron: make sure it's clean otherwise it will mark your fabric.

Tape measure: for accurate measuring.

Hand sewing needles: you'll always need these, in various sizes to cope with different thicknesses of fabric and thread.

Thimble: this will stop you spiking your finger.

Re-positionable fabric adhesive spray: good for holding appliqué and layers of fabric and wadding in place before sewing – and it won't stick to your needle!

Seam ripper: a useful little tool for ripping open seams – after all, accidents will happen!

Wadding: buy hollow-fibre pillows instead of kapok and use the filling as wadding – much more cost-effective and just as soft.

Pointed wooden tool: good for pushing out corners – saves you reaching for the scissors and piercing your fabric.

Rotary cutter: this is a must-have for crisp, accurate, sharp, straight lines. Use with a cutting mat and rectangular ruler.

Everything shown here is listed opposite – apart from the cup of tea, even though it's just as important! The little heart-shaped pincushion is one of the hearts made in the project on page 90.

Before you start

Here are some useful tips before you start sewing:

- Take your time measuring and cutting fabric. If your stitching is wrong you can always unpick, but if you cut your fabric wrong it could cost you more fabric.
- If you're not too good at sewing in a straight line, put a piece of tape over the flat bed of your sewing machine to use as a guide.
- Change your machine needle after approximately eight hours of sewing; a blunt needle can pucker your fabric.
- Good lighting is essential for successful sewing. Daylight bulbs allow you to see the true colours.
- Always use good-quality thread. There's a time and place for saving money, but don't skimp when it comes to thread! Cheap thread can break easily and shed fibres into your sewing machine.
- Many fabrics nowadays are pre-shrunk, but if you're not sure, wash and dry your fabric before cutting it.
- Ironing is an important part of sewing. Your seams will sit better and you'll have a more professional finish if you iron them as you go. Pre-ironed fabric is easier to work with.
- Always use sharp scissors, and never use your fabric scissors to cut paper as it will blunt them.

A piece of tape stuck down on the flat bed of your machine as shown will help you sew in a straight line.

Some simple stitches

Familiarise yourself with the following stitches and, though really simple to learn, they will give your sewing project a neat, professional finish.

APPLIQUÉ

Set your sewing machine to a wide zigzag stitch and test on a piece of scrap fabric – you may prefer a narrower stitch. Centre the edge of the shape under the middle of your satin-stitch foot, and gently guide it under the foot. Don't push or pull as the fabric will distort. Stitch all the way around the shape.

A satin-stitch foot has two ski-like bars underneath that raise the foot up slightly, allowing the dense stitches to pass underneath easily.

If you find you've sewn just inside your appliqué shape, use duck-billed scissors to trim away the excess fabric accurately.

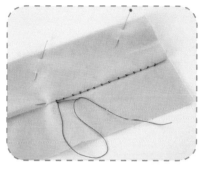

SLIP STITCH

I use this for my bias binding. The tiny stitches are barely visible.

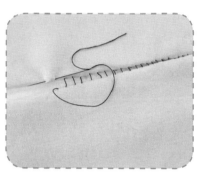

LADDER STITCH

An invisible stitch used to close openings from the right side of the fabric.

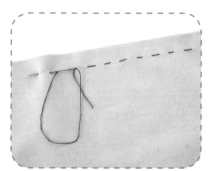

TACKING STITCH

Also known as basting stitch, this is a large running stitch used to hold fabric in place temporarily and then unpicked after machine stitching. It is also used to gather fabric, as in the rosette on the headband (page 62).

FRENCH KNOTS

This stitch results in a little knot that can be used for decoration. It also makes very good beady eyes, as on the chicken doorstop (page 56).

1 Knot your thread and insert your needle from the back of your fabric. Make a tiny stitch, but before pulling the needle all the way through, wrap the thread around it three or four times as shown.

2 Hold the base of the knot and gently ease the needle through. Stab the fabric in the same spot as you first came through and take the needle through to the back of the work. Pull the thread and it will form a tight knot on the surface.

3 If you're making several knots, take your needle to the next position and carry on.

Bias binding

I only realised after writing this book just how much bias binding I use, so I thought I'd explain what it is, why I use it, and how to apply it.

If you look at a piece of woven fabric, the weave goes up and down, and across. The up-and-down threads are the warp, and the across threads are the weft. If you pull on the fabric, it won't stretch. Now, turn the fabric to a 45° angle and pull. It should now stretch. Bias-binding tape is a woven fabric cut into strips at a 45° angle. This means it will stretch around curves and, secondly, it won't fray.

Bias-binding tape is useful for edging curves and gives any item a professional finish. You'll see in this book the difference it makes to projects like the craft caddy, apron, peg bag, oven gloves and many more.

This pretty book bag (page 16) has been edged with bias binding in a coordinating colour and adorned with ribbon handles and buttons for a stylish look.

APPLYING BIAS BINDING ALONG A STRAIGHT EDGE

Bias-binding tape comes in a long strip that is pre-pressed in half, with the raw edges meeting in the centre.

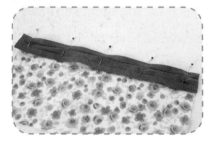

1 With right sides facing, lay the tape along the edge of the fabric, open up one side and pin the two raw edges together.

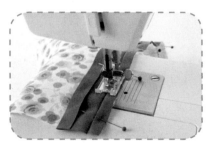

2 Sew the tape to the fabric along the pre-ironed crease.

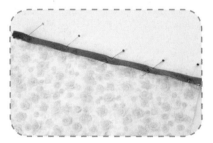

3 If you need to trim off a bulky hem, now is the time to do it. Then fold the tape over the edge of the fabric and pin. neatly in place.

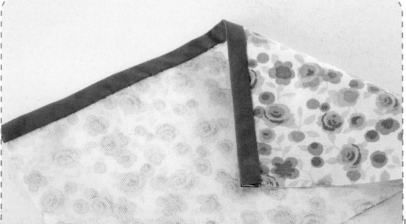

4 Two choices now: to make the stitches invisible, slip stitch the back of the bias-binding tape to your fabric, or, for speed, carefully sew along the edge from the right side using your sewing machine.

APPLYING BIAS BINDING AROUND A CIRCLE

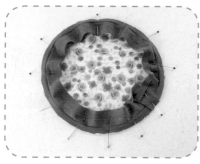

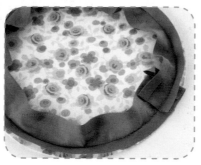

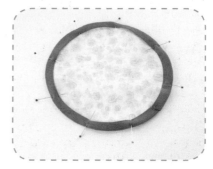

1 Fold in the end of the bias-binding tape by about ¼in (0.5cm), then pin it to the circle of fabric, right sides facing, easing the tape gently so it doesn't pucker. When the end of the tape meets the beginning, simply lay it over the folded end.

2 Sew along the pre-ironed crease, making sure you line up the stitching at the beginning and end.

3 Fold the binding over the raw edge and pin then stitch in place, using either slip stitch or machine stitch.

USING BIAS BINDING WITH PIPING

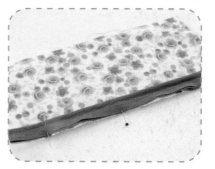

1 Iron the bias-binding tape flat. Fold it in half and sandwich the piping in the middle. Pin in place.

2 Using the zipper foot, sew the two sides of the tape together, close to the piping as shown in the image.

3 Lay the tape on the right side of the fabric with the two raw edges together, as shown, then sew the tape to the fabric just outside the previous stitch line.

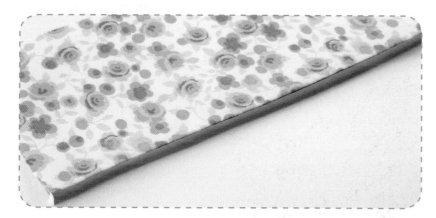

4 Turn and press. If you wish, you could topstitch alongside the piping to secure the seam.

Book Bag

If you're giving a book as a gift, what a lovely way to dress it up! Here is a practical, easy way to carry your holiday reading to the beach, or your text book to college.

What you need

A piece of cotton fabric approximately 3 times the width of your book cover when closed, and at least 2in (5cm) higher

The same size of lining fabric

About 30in (76cm) of coordinating bias-binding tape

Two strips of ribbon for handles, 6in (15cm) each in length

A length of ribbon for a bookmark, 2in (5cm) longer than your page, and a small matching bow

Curtain ring

Buttons to embellish

1 First, measure your book. Begin by taking the tape measure all the way around your book, then add 9in (23cm).

2 Next, measure the height of your book and add 2in (5cm).

3 Cut both your fabric and the lining to this size. Pin or tack the lining and fabric together, right sides out, with raw edges matching.

4 Apply the bias tape to the shorter edges (see page 14).

5 Fold these edges in by 4in (10cm) and press the folds to mark them.

6 For the bookmark, thread the end of the ribbon through a curtain ring and stitch it in place by hand, then glue a little bow on top to cover the stitches.

7 Fold the entire piece in half and mark the centre point with a pin, then tack the bookmark ribbon to this point.

8 Refold the ends (see step 5) and add the remaining bias tape to the raw edges at the top and bottom.

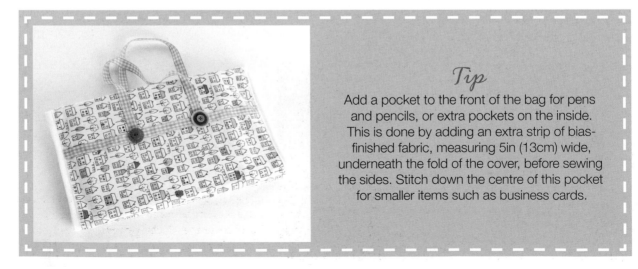

Tip

Add a pocket to the front of the bag for pens and pencils, or extra pockets on the inside. This is done by adding an extra strip of bias-finished fabric, measuring 5in (13cm) wide, underneath the fold of the cover, before sewing the sides. Stitch down the centre of this pocket for smaller items such as business cards.

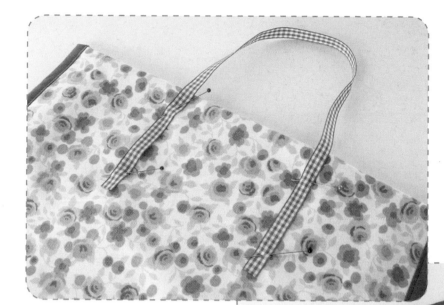

9 Place the cover of the book into the pockets you've just made, and mark the position you'd like for the handles. Make sure the distance between the sides of the book cover and the ribbon is equal.

Tip
You could make the handles using fabric, in the same way as the sewing machine dust-cover handle (page 88).

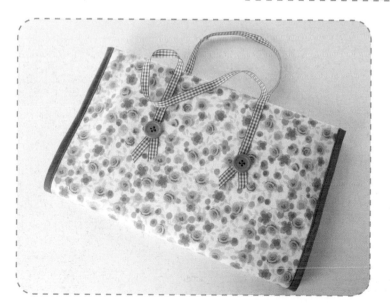

10 Sew the ribbon on securely, by stitching in a cross. Fold short pieces of ribbon and place them at the ends of the handles, and cover the stitches with buttons for a finishing touch.

Wet-wipe Sachet Cover

Every parent or pet owner knows how useful wet wipes can be when you are out and about for cleaning sticky fingers or muddy paws! So why not pop the sachet inside one of these easy-to-make covers and transform it into a stylish accessory?

What you need

A piece of cotton fabric approximately 12in (30.5cm) square

24in (61cm) of bias-binding tape

Ribbon and buttons to decorate

Tip

Cotton is ideal, but try other non-stretch fabrics like felt. The cover at the back in the picture below was a fabric I felted myself using brightly coloured yarn and a felting machine.

1 Measure the height of your wet-wipe sachet and add 1in (2.5cm). Measure the width of the packet and times it by two. Cut your fabric to this size.

2 Edge the two shorter sides with bias tape.

3 Measure the centre point of the bound edges, and sew a ribbon fastening to each one on the wrong side of the fabric. Cover the stitching with buttons on the right side.

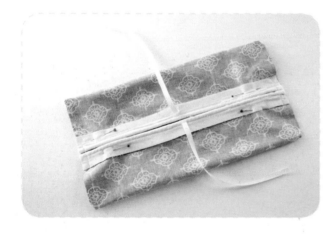

4 Fold the fabric in half widthways and mark the centre point with a pin at each end; unfold.

5 With the fabric face up, fold both bound edges together to meet in the middle, at the pin marks, and pin.

6 Sew across both ends and snip the seam allowances at the corners for each.

Tip
One long ribbon tied all the way around would give the cover a gift-like appearance.

7 Turn the cover right side out.

Tote Bag

This handy shopper is stylish as well as practical, and has pockets on the front to help keep you organised. I used curtain-weight cotton as it is durable and helps the bag keep its shape.

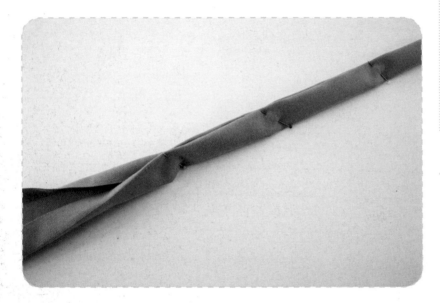

1 First, make the handles. Fold the long strips of lining fabric in half lengthways and press. Then fold the long outer edges to meet in the centre, pin, press and sew. These should now look like two large pieces of bias binding.

2 Lay the two main pieces of the bag flat, right sides up, and pin then stitch the handles in place on each piece. Position the handles so they are an even distance from the two outer edges of the bag, and facing inwards towards the fabric, as shown.

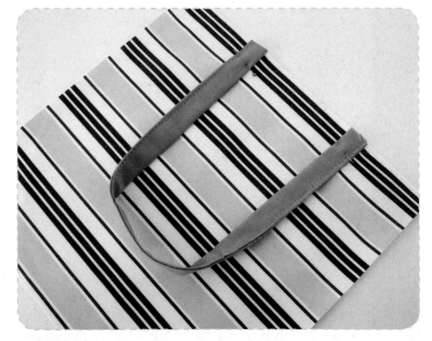

3 The pocket is next. First apply the bias binding across the top of the pocket (see page 14).

4 Fold under the bottom of the pocket and press.

5 Pin then sew the pocket across the front of the bag on three sides, leaving the top, bound edge, open.

6 Sew straight down the front of the pocket, centrally, to divide the pocket into two. Make sure you back-tack at the top for strength.

7 Take the lining pieces and sew the shorter sides to the top of the bag pieces, making sure the handles are caught in the seam.

8 Put the front and back pieces of the bag together, right sides facing, making sure the seams meet. Pin then sew all the way round, leaving a gap of around 4in (10cm) at the bottom of the lining for turning.

9 Before turning, take the bottom corners of the bag and pinch them open. You will be able to match the bottom seam to the side seam by feeling the ridge of the seams and putting them together. Pin and sew across the corner, 2in (5cm) from the point.

10 Do this for all four corners, then cut off the excess fabric. This will shape the base of the bag.

11 Turn the bag right side out, then hand stitch across the turning gap in the lining. As the lining fabric was longer than the outer patterned fabric, when you turn, there will be a little lining exposed. Use this to make a border across the top of the bag. Press, and shop!

Make-up Bag

This useful little bag is great for keeping your make-up or bathroom bits and pieces tidy. Use fabric that coordinates with your bathroom or bedroom décor, or make one to match your favourite suitcase or travel bag for when you're on the move. If applying motifs, appliqué them before you put the bag together (see page 12).

(see page 12)

What you need

Two rectangles of patterned cotton fabric, 10 x 7in (25.5 x 18cm)

One long rectangle of contrasting fabric, 3½ x 36in (9 x 91.5cm)

8in (20.5cm) zip (you could make the opening wider by using a longer zip)

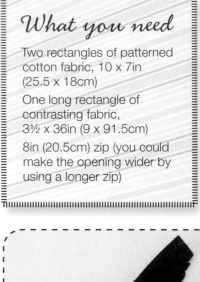

1 First, fit the zip. Take a 9in (23cm) strip of the long length of fabric and cut it in half lengthways. Fit the zip by stitching one strip to each side of the zip with right sides facing.

2 Cut the remaining long strip in two. Sew one of these lengths to each end of the zip. If the zipped section is then a little wider, simply trim off the excess.

3 Place the zipped section centrally on top of one of the patterned pieces of fabric, right sides together. Pin then sew it to the patterned fabric. Start sewing from the zip, across the top, down one side and along the bottom, stopping at the centre bottom. Turn the bag over and sew around the other side until your stitches meet at the bottom of the bag. You will have a little extra fabric here, but don't trim it off yet.

4 Repeat with the other piece of patterned fabric to make the other side of the bag.

5 Now sew across the opening at the bottom of the bag and trim off the excess fabric. Turn the bag the right way out and press it neatly.

Tip
To help stop fraying, sew a zigzag stitch all around the seams.

Child's Apron

This pretty apron will help protect your child's clothing from cake mixture in the kitchen as well as paint splashes! You could match the fabric to your kitchen décor or go for a favourite colour or cartoon character.

What you need

18 x 15in (46 x 38cm) of fabric

12 x 7½in (30.5 x 19cm) of contrasting fabric for the pocket

12in (30.5cm) of bias-binding tape for the top of the pocket

1.5yd (1.4m) of tape for ties

Two large buttons

1 Measure a rectangle of cotton fabric, 15in (38cm) long by 18in (46cm) wide. If your fabric is patterned, make sure the pattern is the right way up!

2 Fold the fabric in half lengthways, and mark with a disappearing pen 6¼in (16cm) along the top from the open side, and 9in (23cm) down. Draw a diagonal line joining the two marks and cut across the corner.

Tips

You could vary the size of the apron depending on the size of the child. Simply measure the child from the chest to just above the knee for the length, and from one side of the waist to the other for the width.

Instead of hemming the apron, you could apply bias binding all the way round, or decorate with ric-rac or a similar trimming.

3 Fold over a ½in (1cm) hem twice all the way round, pin then topstitch it in place. Press.

4 Take the piece of fabric measuring 12 x 7½in (30.5 x 19cm) for the pocket and sew bias binding across the top (see page 14).

(see page 14)

Tip

If you decide to use wipeable, coated fabric like oilcloth, you won't need to hem. Make sure the coated side is uppermost when putting it through the sewing machine because it tends to jam a little if face down.

5 Fold the pocket in half to find the centre point and mark it with a pin. Do the same with the apron, and place the pocket in the centre of the apron.

6 Fold in the three remaining edges of the pocket once, by around ½in (1cm), and pin in place.

7 Topstitch around these three sides, back-tacking at the top of the pocket to re-enforce the corners. To divide the pocket in two, stitch down the centre mark and, again, press.

8 For the straps, cut two lengths of tape, each around 18in (46cm) long, and attach them to the waist of the apron. You may need to hem the ends of the tape to stop them fraying.

9 For the neck strap, cut another piece of the tape, around 15¾in (40cm) long, and stitch it at an angle to the top of one side of the apron. If you can, try the apron on before attaching the other side, again at an angle, so you have a perfect fit.

10 To make the joins a little neater, sew a button over them. This also adds a decorative touch.

Heart-shaped variation

The pocket doesn't have to be rectangular; try a sweet heart-shaped pocket for a feminine finish.

1 You'll need two heart shapes. Sew them together, right sides facing, and leave a gap for turning.

2 Turn right side out and press, then topstitch around the top of the heart. Topstitch the pocket to the apron, to one side of the centre mark, leaving the top open.

Make-up Brush Roll

Keep your make-up brushes tidy with this practical brush holder. Use fabric that matches the tote bag on page 22 for a coordinated set. If you are a budding artist, this useful roll will keep your paintbrushes handy too!

What you need

Two pieces of fabric measuring 12 x 10in (30.5 x 25.5cm)

One strip of fabric approximately 36 x 4in (91.5 x 10cm)

Approximately 2yd (1.9m) of bias-binding tape

About 18in (46cm) of ribbon to tie

Fabric adhesive spray

Tip

Using a striped fabric for the pockets makes them easy to sew by just following the lines!

1 Cut your pieces of fabric to the correct size. If necessary, measure the length of your longest brush and cut your fabric about 2in (5cm) longer than this. 10in (25.5cm) should be long enough to accommodate a brush 8in (20.5cm) long. I have used two contrasting fabrics for the two sides of the roll, and one of these for the little pockets.

2 Spray fabric adhesive to the two large pieces of the roll wrong sides together, or pin and tack all the way around to hold them in place.

3 Gently round off the corners either freehand (if you're confident) or by drawing an arc around a teacup for an accurate curve.

4 Edge the long side of the fabric for the pocket with bias binding.

5 Lay the roll face down and position the pocket on the lower part, face up. Sew the two together down the left-hand side.

6 Put one of your brushes in place and pin just to the right of it to make a long pocket that it will fit into comfortably.

7 Continue to measure and make pockets all the way across the roll.

8 Sew with a straight stitch along all the pin marks to make the pockets, back-tacking at the top of each one to strengthen them. Cut off any excess fabric from the long strip, keeping the shape of the rounded corners.

9 Sew along the bottom of the pockets, flattening them and keeping your stitches as close to the edge as possible so they'll be covered by the bias binding.

10 Sew bias binding all the way around the roll.

11 Find the centre of the ribbon and stitch this to the centre back of the roll, as shown in the image.

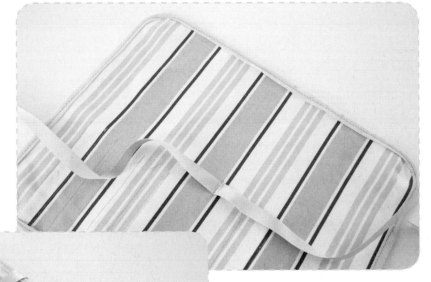

The completed roll can be secured by tying the ribbon ends in a bow.

Ringing the changes

Simply by changing the dimensions, the roll becomes a handy store for your knitting needles.

Peg Bag

Hang this pretty peg bag on the washing line, buy some new pegs to go with it, and hanging out the washing will no longer be just another boring household chore! Or try popping your cleaning products in it and hanging it behind the kitchen door.

What you need

Wooden coat hanger

Two pieces of fabric 16¾ x 12in (42.5 x 30.5cm), or ¾in (2cm) wider than the hanger

Two strips of bias-binding tape the same width as the fabric

A button and ribbon about 4in (10cm) long for the fastening

1 Lay the two pieces of fabric right sides together.

2 Place the coat hanger at the top of the fabric and draw across the arc, leaving a gap where the hanger hook is. Cut ½in (1cm) above this line.

3 Draw a line across one piece of fabric 7in (18cm) up from the bottom and cut along the line.

4 Apply bias binding across the cut edge of both pieces.

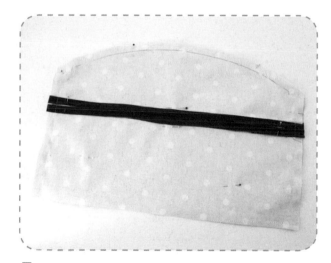

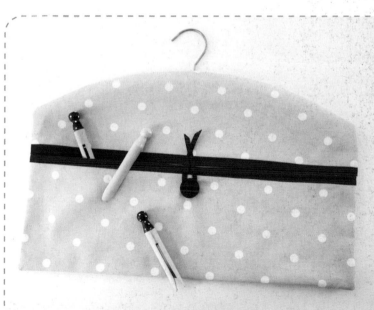

5 Place these two pieces face down on top of the remaining piece of fabric, and pin the layers together.

6 Sew all the way around the edge, leaving a gap of ¼in (0.5cm) for the hanger hook. Back-tack on each side of this gap to strengthen the hole.

7 Snip across the corners in the seam allowances at the bottom of the bag to reduce bulk.

8 Turn the bag the right way out and press. Measure and mark the centre of the opening and sew your button just below it. Make a loop from the ribbon and sew it to the top section so that it fits around the button to fasten. Insert the coat hanger, working the hook carefully through the hole at the top.

Pocket Apron

This useful apron will keep your gardening tools in order and leave your hands free for tending the plants. And it can be adapted easily for the painter, cleaner and certainly the stitcher!

What you need

One piece of fabric measuring 18 x 9in (46 x 23cm)

Iron-on interfacing (if using light cotton fabric)

For the pocket, around 18 x 6in (46 x 15cm) of fabric

Approximately 2yd (1.9m) of bias-binding tape

Ribbon tape for the tie measuring approximately 1½yd (1.4m)

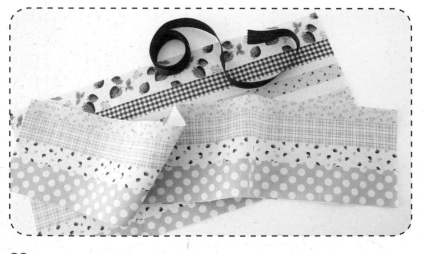

A useful place to store your scissors, pins, threads, buttons and other sewing paraphernalia.

1 Gather together the fabric and trimmings you need to make the apron. If you're using a lightweight cotton fabric, back it with iron-on interfacing to add a little weight.

Tip
Use oilcloth for a wipe-clean apron, or add a frill for a really feminine look.

2 Sew bias binding across the top of the 18in (46cm) length of pocket.

3 Divide the pocket into four equal sections: fold the pocket in half and mark the fold line with a disappearing pen, then fold again and mark the quarters with the pen.

4 Place the pocket, right side up, across the lower part of the apron and pin the edges together. If the pocket is slightly larger than the apron, cut off the excess fabric so they are exactly the same size.

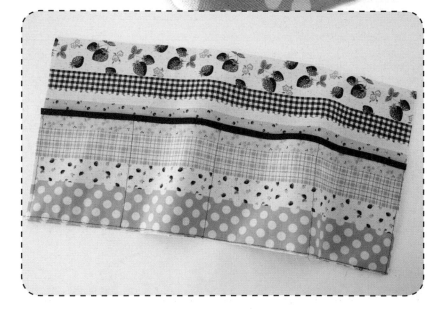

5 Sew down both sides and across the bottom of the pocket, quite close to the edge so that the stitches will be concealed under the bias tape. Topstitch the individual pockets along your marked lines.

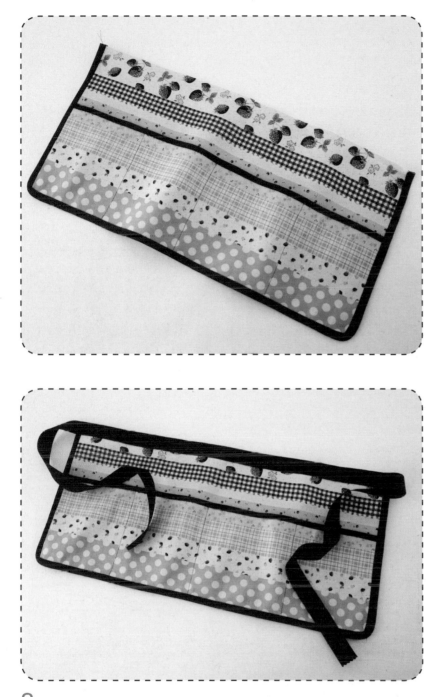

6 Curve the bottom two corners to make binding easier. If you're not too confident freehand, draw an arc using something like an egg-cup or small glass as a template.

7 Sew the bias-binding tape around three sides of the apron, excluding the top (see page 14).

8 Fold your ribbon tape in half widthways and mark the centre point with a pin, then lay the ribbon across the top of the apron, aligning this point with the centre top of the apron. Pin the ribbon in place.

9 Make sure the top edge of the ribbon is aligned with the top edge of the apron and sew along the top of the ribbon to attach it to the apron. Then sew across the bottom of the ribbon to secure it.

Glasses Case

This pretty glasses case is padded and lined with soft cotton to protect the lenses. What a lovely gift this would make, and a trendy holder for your sunglasses too! Make the case larger for a laptop or tablet, or smaller for a phone case.

What you need

Cotton fabric measuring 12 x 9in (30.5 x 23cm)

Cotton lining fabric to the same measurement

Wadding, cut to the same measurement

Approximately 1yd (1m) of bias-binding tape

Fabric adhesive spray

This cool case is perfect for keeping your sunglasses or reading glasses safe and scratch-free.

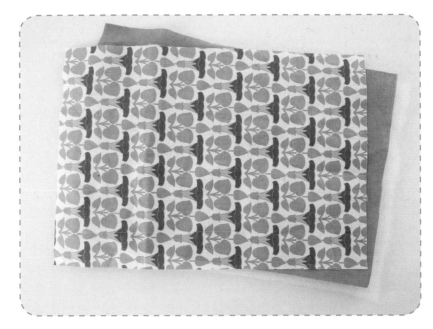

1 Cut a piece of fabric, one of lining and one of wadding, all measuring 9in (23cm) wide and 12in (30.5cm) long. If your fabric has a pattern with a distinct top and bottom, like the one used here, make sure you cut it the right way.

2 Use temporary fabric spray to hold all three layers together, with the wadding in the centre.

3 Lay the fabric with a long edge at the top and make a stitch line 3in (7.5cm) from the right-hand side, through all three layers. (The bottom edge of the fabric design should be on this right edge.) This will help the fastening flap to fold neatly.

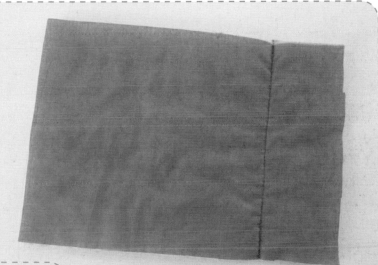

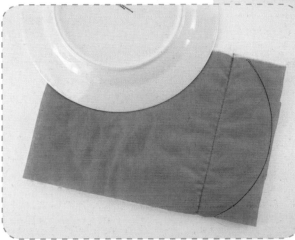

4 Draw round a small plate to make a curve at the right-hand end of the rectangle, to the right of the stitched line, and cut out the rounded shape.

5 Edge the opposite short side with bias binding (see page 14).

6 Fold this edge over to meet the stitch line, pin, then sew both sides of the case as close to the edge as you can. You'll see that the case is now taking shape.

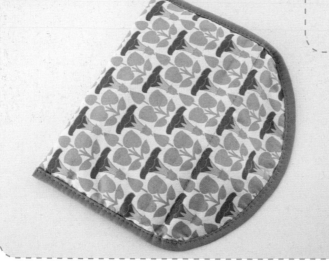

7 Apply bias binding all the way around the edge of the case.

8 To fasten the case, I sewed a button to the centre front, then made a loop from matching ribbon and stitched it to the flap, then covered my stitching with a bow. You could use Velcro dots fo the fastening instead of a button, or try one of those magnetic fasteners you can buy for handbags. Or a ribbon bow tied all around the case would look gorgeous!

Craft Caddy

Keep your craft goodies neat and tidy with this colourful organiser. You'll find numerous other uses for this handy holder too – try making it using oilcloth for a wipe-clean finish, or make a matching picnic mat and use it to carry your food, plates and cutlery for a stylish summer picnic. You could make the caddy larger in size, but you may need to use interfacing to stiffen the panels.

What you need

Four pieces of cotton fabric, each measuring 5 x 6in (13 x 15cm)

Four pieces of contrasting cotton for lining, measuring 5 x 6in (13 x 15cm)

One square of each fabric for the base, measuring 5in (13cm) square

For the pockets, four pieces of lining fabric measuring 6½ x 4in (16.5 x 10cm)

20in (51cm) of bias-binding tape

8in (20.5cm) of ribbon or cord for the handles

Four buttons

1 Using fabric adhesive spray, stick each side panel to a piece of lining fabric, wrong sides together. Do the same with the square base.

2 Take the four pocket pieces and fold them in half lengthways, then press. Embroider or zigzag stitch along the folded edge.

3 Fold each pocket piece in half and mark the centre line by creasing with your fingers.

4 Take the side panels, and mark the halfway line in the same way.

5 Place a pocket piece on top of each side panel, pin, then sew straight down the centre, remembering to back-tack each end of your stitching to secure.

6 For each panel, match the raw edges of the pocket piece to the edges of the side panel, pin, then sew as close to the edges as you can. You will start to see the pockets taking shape!

7 Pinch the bottom of each pocket in the centre and pin the dart in place. Sew across the base of the pockets, again close to the edge. Do this with all four panels.

8 Place two panels together, with the pockets on the inside, and sew down one side. Trim the seam as close to the stitches as you can, without cutting through the line of stitching.

9 Open up the seam, turn over, and sew over the top of the seam from the right side. This should enclose the raw edge of the seam to make it neat. This is how it should look from the outside ...

10 ... and this is the inside.

11 Repeat this with all four seams until you have a complete box shape.

12 Now to attach the base! With your box inside out, place the base of the caddy inside and pin one edge to the box. Sew across this edge first. If you're confident, leave the needle in the down position when you get to the corner, lift the presser foot and turn the fabric, pull the edges together and sew to the next corner before repeating. If you find it easier, just sew one side at a time, stopping and re-pinning after each side is sewn.

13 To neaten the seam, sew over the join with a zigzag or overcasting stitch.

14 Turn the caddy in the right way.

15 Apply the bias binding all the way around the top of the caddy (see page 14).

16 Measure the centre point of two opposite sides and attach ribbon or cord handles either side of this point by hand. Cover up the ends of the handles with buttons.

Neck Cushion

Stay comfortable and cosy on long journeys (or on the sofa!) with this padded neck rest. To make the cushion really cosy, try using fleece fabric or a brushed cotton.

What you need

Two pieces of coordinating fabrics, each 12in (30.5cm) square
Wadding

1 To make the cushion shape, first lay the two pieces of fabric together with right sides facing and draw a circle on to the fabric around a large plate or round chopping board, measuring approximately 12in (30.5cm) across. Cut it out.

2 Draw a second circle in the middle of the first approximately 4in (10cm) across. Fold the circle in half and cut out the inner circle.

3 Unfold the circle and cut a section approximately 4in (10cm) across out of the ring and round off the edges.

4 Sew all the way around with a small straight stitch, leaving a gap of around 2in (5cm) for turning.

5 Turn, and stuff with wadding so that the cushion is really firm.

6 Hand stitch the opening with a ladder stitch to close (see page 13).

The finished cushion.

Owl and Pussy Cat

I started making this wise old owl, but as it developed I realised it could just as easily be a cat! Both make great ornaments to decorate your home. Try weighting them with rice, sand or craft pellets and use them as doorstops.

For the owl

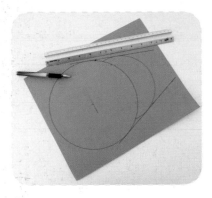

1 Draw around the large plate on the card as shown.

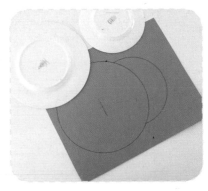

2 Place the smaller plate just over the edge of the circle and draw around it to form a head shape.

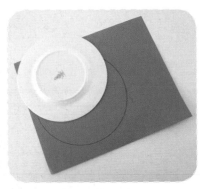

3 Extend the sides of the two circles upwards with a ruler, about 2in (5cm) beyond the smaller circle. These will be the ears.

4 As in the picture above, bring the extended lines down to make triangular ears, and cut out the template.

What you need

For the owl:

Two pieces of cotton fabric for the body, measuring 11 x 9in (28 x 23cm) This could be one piece or a patchwork of fabrics

For the wings, four pieces of contrasting fabric measuring 5 x 3in (13 x 7.5cm)

Triangle of plain fabric for the beak, 2½in (6.5cm) across the base

Buttons for eyes

½yd (0.5m) ribbon for feet

Wadding

Card and two plates, 8in (20.5cm) and 6in (15cm) across, to make a template

For the cat:

Two pieces of cotton fabric for the body, (as for the owl)

Buttons for eyes

Contrasting thread for the nose and whiskers

Two circles of fabric for the cheeks, about 2in (5cm) in diameter

Four U-shaped pieces of fabric for the feet, measuring about 3 x 2in (7.5 x 5cm)

Wadding

Card and two plates, (as for the owl template)

4in (10cm) ribbon for the bow

Tip

Be careful if you are giving the owl or the pussy cat as a gift to youngsters. You may wish to embroider the eyes instead.

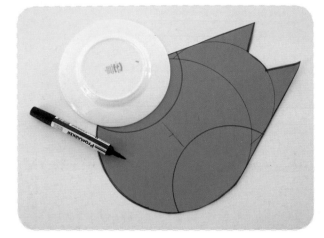

5 Take the smaller of the two plates and draw an outline of the wings on each side of the owl's body.

6 Use the template to cut two pieces of the main fabric for the body, then cut out the wing shapes from the template and cut four of these from the wing fabric.

7 Place two wings on either side of the body, front and back. Make sure the two sides match up. Stitch these in place with a narrow satin stitch (zigzag).

8 Sew the buttons in place on the front of the owl for eyes. Give him character by placing them close together, and line up the holes so they are symmetrical.

9 Satin stitch the triangular beak on, just below the eyes.

10 For the feet, cut the ribbon into six equal pieces. Loop each piece in half. Take the front of the owl and pin three on either side at the base. Angle them so they point outwards.

11 Tack the ribbons in place and remove the pins.

12 Place both sides of the owl face to face and sew all around the edge, leaving a gap in between the feet for turning the fabric out.

13 Turn the owl the right way out and stuff with wadding.

14 Hand stitch the opening closed.

For the cat

To make the cat, a few things need to change: the face, the tail, the nose and the feet.

1 You can still use buttons for eyes, but give him two round cheeks, which are satin stitched on to the face, and use long straight stitches to make whiskers.

2 Mark a small triangle with pen for a nose, then stitch over it with a coordinating thread.

3 No wings this time, and the cat has two little feet made from U-shaped pieces of stuffed fabric, stitched through when stuffed to make little toes.

4 The cat's tail is simply a tube of fabric with a knot in the end. To finish, add a little bow, hand sewn to the base of the tail.

Try using different buttons, fabrics and so on to vary the characters of your toys. You'll be amazed how different they can look just by moving a button here or adding some pointy eyebrows!

Chicken Doorstop

Chickens have so much personality, and this little lady is no exception. She's useful for keeping your doors open and looks great in the kitchen – and she isn't egg-xactly difficult to make either ... Try making smaller chickens for Easter decorations, and use beads or buttons for eyes.

What you need

Two pieces of cotton fabric, each measuring 16 x 12in (40.5 x 30.5cm)

Small pieces of contrasting fabric for the wings

Card and a side plate to make a template

Red ribbon for comb, tail feathers, wattle and feet.

Red yarn for eyes

Wadding

A pouch of rice, sand or craft pellets to add weight

Repositionable fabric adhesive spray

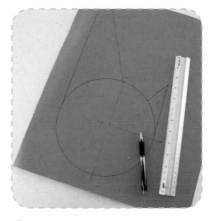

1 Draw a circle around the side plate at the lower end of your piece of card.

2 Mark the centre of the circle by drawing a cross. From the outer left edge draw a straight line 8in (20.5cm) upwards, and from the opposite side draw a line upwards measuring around 4in (10cm).

3 Join the longer line to the top centre of the circle to make a triangle, then join the shorter line to the circle to make a smaller triangle. You should be able to see the chicken starting to take shape now.

4 Take a marker pen and draw around the outline of the chicken, rounding off the corners. Draw a semi-circle where the wings will be going. (Use a mug or small bowl for the curve if you're not confident at drawing freehand.) Draw a straight line across the bottom to help the chicken stand when finished.

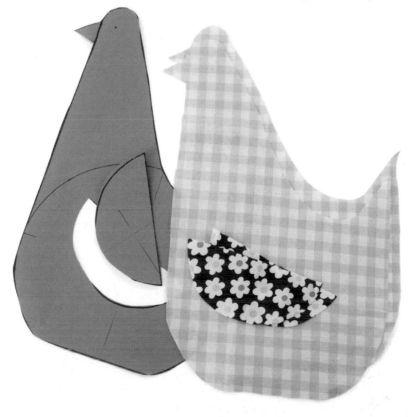

5 Cut out the shape of the wing from the pattern. Now transfer the patterns to the fabric and cut them out. You will need two bodies and two wings. If your fabrics have a definite right and wrong side, flip your patterns to cut the second pieces.

6 Secure the wings to the body with repositionable fabric adhesive spray, making sure both sides are symmetrical, and satin stitch all the way round.

7 Cut the ribbon into 4in (10cm) lengths and loop, then pin and tack the tail feathers, comb and wattle in place, as shown.

Tip

If the ribbon tail, wattle and comb don't work easily, hand sew them on afterwards, as you will for the feet.

8 Pin the two sides of the chicken together, right sides facing, then sew all the way round, keeping the tail, wattle and comb tucked in. Leave a gap of around 4in (10cm) across the base for turning.

9 Turn the chicken the right way out and stuff tightly with wadding. Before sewing across the base, push the pouch of rice, sand or craft pellets into the bottom.

10 Loop more ribbon into threes for the feet, and hand sew them to the base of the doorstop.

11 For the eyes, thread red yarn through a large needle and push the needle into the chicken at the back of the neck, pulling the yarn into the neck so it's not seen.

12 Direct the needle to the eye area and pull through both sides of the head. Tie a French knot on each side, pulling tight to make a 'dimpled' effect as show on the right.

Padded Coat Hanger

This pretty coat hanger will not only look lovely in your closet, it actually helps maintain the shape of your garments and stops them slipping on to the floor.

What you need

Wooden coat hanger

Two pieces of fabric, each measuring 19 x 5in (48 x 13cm) – this works with a coat hanger that measures 16in (40.5cm) across

Wadding cut into 2in (5cm) strips

Ribbon for trimming

Fabric adhesive spray

1 Lay your two pieces of fabric right sides together.

2 Lay the coat hanger on the top part of the fabric so that the hook is approximately ½in (1cm) in from the edge. Draw around half the hanger, leaving a border of ½in (1cm).

3 Cut out these shapes, then repeat on the lower part of the fabric. You should have four shapes altogether.

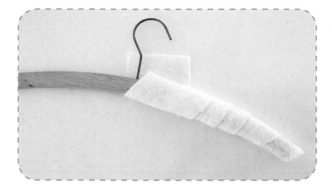

4 Spray the hanger with fabric adhesive, then wrap the strips of wadding around it.

5 Put an extra square of wadding over the ends of the hanger as shown above.

6 Place the cut-out pieces right sides together, pin, then sew all the way round leaving the short straight end open. Turn the right way out and press. You will now have two matching 'sleeves'.

Tip

Make sure you glue the wadding to the hanger, otherwise it will 'scrunch up' when pulling the sleeve of fabric over it.

7 Slip the fabric sleeves over each side of the hanger.

Tip

If you're a dressmaker, how about matching your hangers with leftover dress fabric?

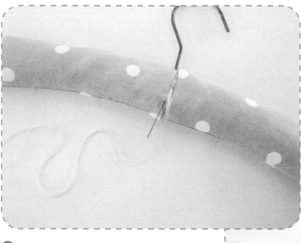

8 Fold in the fabric at the join, then hand stitch the two sleeves together. Don't worry too much about stitching neatly as this will be covered by ribbon.

9 Glue a piece of decorative ribbon over your stitches, and finish off with a little bow. If you like, pop a little fabric adhesive on to the hook and wrap ribbon around it to finish.

Rosette Headband

A pretty cotton headband that any little (or big!) girl would look lovely wearing.

1 Take the two strips of floral fabric and fold them in half lengthways. Pin then sew along the long edge taking a ¼in (0.5cm) seam allowance.

2 Turn each strip the right way out then re-fold and press with the seam in the centre back of the rectangle.

3 Thread the elastic through the narrower strip by attaching a safety pin to one end and pulling through, then secure each end with a few stitches. The fabric should gather up.

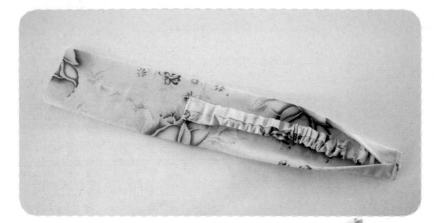

4 Lay out the larger band of fabric with the seam facing down. Place the elasticated band on top with the seam facing upwards. Wrap one end of the large piece around the smaller one, pin then sew across the end a few times. Snip off the excess fabric.

5 Repeat step 4 on the other end of the headband, then turn the band the right way out.

6 For the rosette, cut one edge of the strip of fabric with pinking shears to stop it from fraying. Choose two contrasting buttons of different sizes.

7 Sew the two short ends of the strip together to make a loop.

8 On the opposite edge to the pinked edge, work running stitch by hand all the way around. The stitches should be even and around ¼in (0.5cm) in length. Don't fasten off the thread at either end.

9 Pull the ends of your thread to gather the fabric, and secure with a knot.

10 Attach the buttons to the centre of the rosette by sewing straight through the centre of both and into the middle of the rosette.

11 Attach the rosette to the headband with a few hand stitches, or see the tip below.

Tip

Stitch a safety pin to the back of the rosette so that it can be removed and worn as a brooch.

Place Mat

This mat is so quick and easy, and can be coordinated with your tablecloth and napkins for a stylish look. Make the mat longer to create a table runner, and sew a tassel in each corner for an expensive look.

What you need

Two pieces of coordinating fabric, each 16 x 10in (40.5 x 25.5cm)

One piece of wadding, 16 x 10¼in (40.5 x 26cm)

1yd (1m) of bias-binding tape

Fabric adhesive spray

1 Layer the two pieces of fabric with the wadding in between and use fabric adhesive spray to stick the layers together. If you wish, tack around the edges with a long straight stitch to secure.

2 Mark the long edges into quarters, then use a disappearing pen to draw diagonal lines across one way then the other so you have diamond shapes all over the fabric.

Tip

The place mat also makes a practical sewing-machine mat to help prevent your work surface from being scratched.

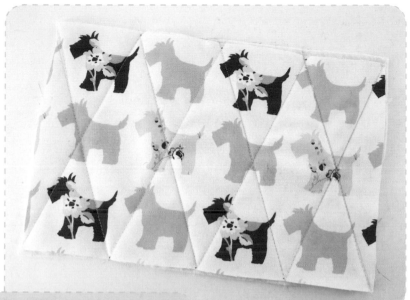

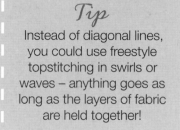

Tip

Instead of diagonal lines, you could use freestyle topstitching in swirls or waves – anything goes as long as the layers of fabric are held together!

3 Use these lines as a guide to topstitch with a long stitch, and quilt the layers together.

Tip

If you use heat-resistant wadding, this mat would make a useful trivet for the kitchen.

4 Apply bias binding to all four sides (see page 14).

Oven Gloves

An affordable way to coordinate your kitchen with matching accessories, these oven gloves are practical as well as pretty! I'd recommend a heavy-weight cotton fabric, the type you'd make curtains with, and the wadding needs to be natural as opposed to polyester to withstand heat. Heat-resistant wadding is available if you shop around.

If you want to add any appliqué, do it after step 4, before the layers are sewn together.

What you need

Two pieces of fabric measuring 34 x 8in (86.5 x 20.5cm)

One length of wadding of the same size

Four pieces of fabric measuring 8 x 9in (20.5 x 23cm)

Two pieces of wadding the same size

2yds (2m) bias binding

8in (20.5cm) side plate for a template

Repositionable fabric adhesive spray

1 Lay one of the long pieces of fabric face down and spray the back with fabric adhesive spray. Lay the wadding on top of this, followed by more fabric adhesive spray, then lay the second long piece of fabric face up on the top.

2 Repeat step 1 with the smaller pieces of fabric. You should now have one long padded 'sandwich' and two smaller ones.

3 Take a side plate and place it at one end of the long strip, with the edge of the plate touching the edge of the fabric. Draw around the arc and cut it out. Repeat this at the other end.

4 Take each of the smaller pieces in turn and round off the one of the shorter edges in the same way. These will form the gloves.

5 Stitch around the edge of each glove, taking a ¼in (0.5cm) seam allowance, and sew bias binding across the straight end of each glove.

6 Stitch all round the long fabric 'sandwich' in the same way as you did for the gloves.

7 Pin the gloves to each end of the centre panel, curved edges matching, then topstitch them together with a long stitch, close to the edge, to secure them firmly for the next step. Sew bias binding all around the edge of the oven gloves.

8 Add a loop of bias binding in the centre of the glove for hanging. It's easier just to hand stitch this in place when the glove is finished, and add a button for decoration if you wish.

Tip
You could quilt together the layers after step 4, by sewing straight lines diagonally over the layers of fabric, or following the pattern of the fabric with your machine. Use a long straight stitch. This is a good way of holding the layers in place if you don't have any fabric adhesive spray.

Notice Board

This useful notice board will keep your notes, shopping lists, photographs or dress patterns to hand, and the pockets can be used to organise scissors, keys or small tools.

1 First, place the canvas in the centre of the fabric and mark the outline on the right side with disappearing pen.

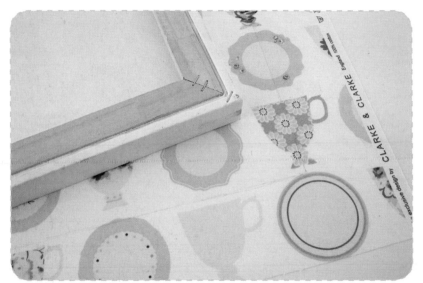

2 Make up the three pockets by sewing the contrasting fabric together in pairs, right sides facing, leaving a small gap for turning. Snip across the corners of the seam allowances, turn the right way out and press.

3 Pleat the bottom of each pocket by folding in the fabric at the sides and pin it in place.

4 Pin the pockets on the left-hand side of the fabric, overlapping them and making sure they sit inside the marked lines. Sew them in place.

5 Turn the fabric over and place the canvas within the marked lines. Fold in the edges to neaten, then staple along one side. Do the same on the opposite side and tighten the fabric as you go. Complete the final two sides.

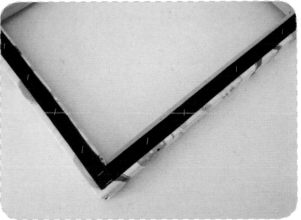

6 Stretch the elastic across the frame, making a diamond pattern, and staple each piece to the back of the frame.

7 If you wish, neaten the back by stapling tape around the frame, as shown.

8 To hang, simply put a tack or two into your wall and hook the frame over it. If you intend to put anything heavy in the pockets you may need to use a screw instead.

Pincushion

This Indian-twist pincushion may look complicated, but it is easier to make than you think. This design could be scaled up easily to make a cushion cover, or you could tie a piece of cord to the pincushion and use it as a scissor keeper.

What you need

Two squares of contrasting fabric, each 7¾ x 7¾in (20 x 20cm)

Wadding

Two buttons or beads

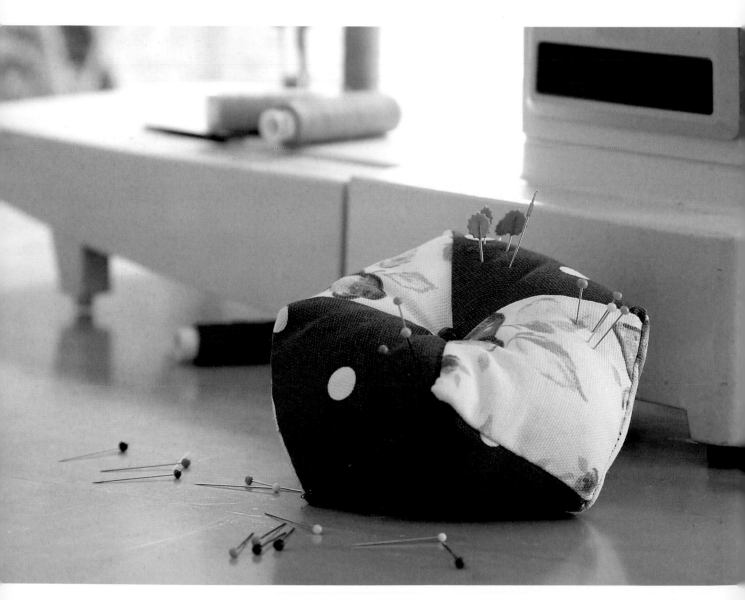

1 Cut both squares into quarters, then sew them back together with alternating designs to make a Battenburg effect, as shown.

2 Place the two squares wrong sides together and rotate the top square by 45°. It should now look like a diamond shape on top of a square.

3 Now flip the pieces so they are right sides together in the same position. Pin or tack the two squares together, matching the points of each one to the seams of the other. Sew, taking a ¼in (0.5cm) seam allowance and leaving a gap for turning. Turn the shape out through the gap.

4 Stuff the pincushion tightly with wadding, and hand sew over the gap with ladder stitch (see page 13).

5 Thread up a long needle, push this straight through the centre of the cushion several times and pull as tight as you can. When the cushion is 'pinched', take the thread through one button or bead placed in the 'dimple' on each side of the pincushion and sew through again to secure.

Slippers

Soft, snuggly and warm, these fleecy slippers are the perfect fit!

What you need

Approximately 12 x 24in (30.5 x 61cm) of fleece fabric

Cotton fabric for the top of the slippers, 12 x 6in (30.5 x 15cm)

Fleece to line the top of the slippers, 12 x 6in 30.5 x 15cm)

12 x 6in (30.5 x 15cm) of thin wadding

24in (61cm) of bias-binding tape

Card and a pen to make a template

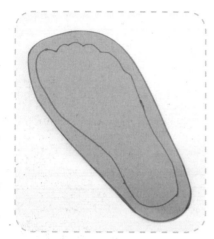

1 To make a template, put your foot on the card and draw round it. Then draw an outline to round off the shape, about ¾in (2cm) wider than your foot all round. Cut around this line.

2 Draw a line across the foot shape abour halfway down. Lay your foot template on to another piece of card and draw around the top half of the foot shape. Then extend the sides out by 1in (2.5cm) on each side to give shape to the top section, as shown above. Cut out this shape.

The templates for the top and bottom pieces of the right slipper. For the left slipper, you will simply turn the templates over.

3 Keeping the templates face up, cut two pieces of fleece and one piece of wadding from the template for the bottom of the slipper, then one piece of fleece, one of wadding and one of cotton fabric from the template for the top of the slipper.

4 Turn the template over, and use it to cut the same pieces. You will now have two symmetrical foot shapes.

5 For the top of each slipper, take the wadding and lay the fleece on top. Place the cotton piece on top of this, face down, and sew across the straight side.

6 Fold the cotton fabric back on top of the wadding, making sure the shapes all match, and topstitch across the folded edge. You could use an embroidery stitch, otherwise a zigzag stitch will be fine. Sew all around the curved side, as close as you can to the edge, to secure all three layers together. Trim off any excess fabric.

7 For each slipper, take the two pieces of fleece for the base and sandwich the wadding in between. Sew all around the outside, close to the edge, to secure all three layers together. Trim away any excess fabric. (Sometimes your wadding can 'grow'. Don't worry about this, just cut away the extra.)

8 Pin the top of the slipper to the base at the centre-front point only.

9 Bring the edges of the top in to meet the edge of the slipper base at the sides, and pin. You should begin to see the slipper taking shape now.

10 Stitch the top to the bottom, close to the edge.

11 Apply bias binding all the way around each slipper. I prefer to finish the bias tape off by hand as there are quite a few layers of fabric now, and it's difficult to get a neat finish with your sewing machine.

> *Tip*
> The bottom of the slippers may be a little slippery! Put a few dots of silicone glue on the base of each slipper, allow to dry overnight and this should help.

79

Coat-hanger Tidy

This handy coat-hanger tidy is useful storage for your crafty stash or tiny children's toys. Make it in pretty floral fabric, add a bow, and it will even look good in the bedroom!

What you need

Wooden coat hanger

Two pieces of fabric measuring 19in (48cm) wide, or 1½in (4cm) wider than your coat hanger, x 8in (20.5cm)

One piece of fabric for the pockets measuring 19 x 4in (48 x 10cm)

½yd (50cm) of bias-binding tape

This coat-hanger tidy is so pretty that you won't want to hide it away in a wardrobe.

Tip

This is a really handy hanger for travelling. Use it to hang blouses and keep matching jewellery or scarves in the pockets.

1 Place the two main pieces of fabric together, wrong sides facing. Place the coat hanger centrally, ½in (1cm) from the top of the fabric. Draw across the arc of the hanger, leaving a gap where the hook goes.

2 Cut the arc shape.

3 Sew bias binding along the top of the pocket fabric. Pin this to the lower part of one of the main fabric pieces, right sides together. Sew along the bottom and down the sides, leaving the top of the pocket open.

4 Divide the long pocket into four quarters by creasing with your fingers, then straight stitch to make four compartments, back-tacking at each end to secure.

5 Place the two sides of the tidy together, right sides facing, and sew up the two sides and across the top, leaving a gap for the coat hanger hook. Leave the bottom open.

6 Turn the piece right sides out, and press. Insert the coat hanger and push the hook through the hole in the top seam.

7 Fold the bottom edges inwards and pin, then topstitch straight across to finish.

Pan Holder

This is a very simple project but is made to look really professional by adding the bias trim. This is where bias-binding tape really comes into its own! Ribbon or fabric cut on the weave wouldn't have the stretch to follow the curve and could pucker.

What you need

Two pieces of fabric, each measuring 9in (23cm) square

One piece of wadding of the same size, preferably heat resistant

26in (66cm) of 1in (2.5cm) wide bias-binding tape

An 8in (20.5cm) diameter side plate to draw around

Fabric adhesive spray

1 Draw around the plate on to both pieces of fabric and the wadding, and cut out the circles.

2 Use fabric adhesive spray to sandwich the three layers together, with the wadding in the middle, then sew the layers together, as close to the edge as you can. (You won't see these stitches when you've finished.)

Tip

I used a curtain-weight fabric, but if you're using a thinner cotton, increase the thickness of your wadding to avoid burnt hands. You could also quilt over the fabrics – do this before applying the bias binding.

3 Open up the binding and place it face down on to the edge of the fabric, folding in the end of the bias tape by about ¼in (0.5cm). Pin, then sew along the crease line with a straight stitch to attach the bias binding to your fabric. When you've completed the circle, overlap the binding at the end by about 1in (2.5cm).

4 Fold the bias-binding tape over the edge of the fabric and pin, making sure the join is lined up and finished neatly. You can hand stitch using a slip stitch to finish so that the stitches aren't too visible, but if you prefer, machine stitch instead. Use a long stitch to reduce puckering.

5 Add a little loop to hang the pan holder up. Fold 2in (5cm) of bias-binding tape in half lengthways and stitch, then fold it in half to make a loop and slip it under the bias edge before sewing. When you've sewn all around the circle attaching the bias-binding tape, fold the loop back on itself and hold it in place with a couple of hand stitches.

Tea Cosy

Keep your teapot warm with this pretty tea cosy. Use fabrics that coordinate with your kitchen décor to add a stylish touch.

Tips

Pop a little loop of ribbon into the top of the cosy for hanging. And of course you can change the size of the cosy to accommodate a larger or smaller teapot!

Adding buttons as decoration is always on trend, or just leave your cosy plain and simple with no embellishments.

1 Lay out the patterned fabric with the longer sides at the top and bottom and place the plate on top, with the edge of the plate touching the top edge. Draw the arc shape then cut it out to make the shape of the tea cosy.

2 Repeat this on the wadding and lining fabric.

3 Sew your appliqué to the right side of one piece of patterned fabric. I cut out the word 'TEA' but you could use a heart shape as shown opposite and described on page 31. Spray the appliqué with re-positionable fabric adhesive before stitching so that the design lies flat.

4 Use a zigzag stitch to outline your design.

5 Lay the patterned fabric face down, spray with fabric adhesive and place the wadding on top.

6 Now turn the fabric over, face up, and lay the lining on top of this. Do not use fabric adhesive this time.

7 Sew across the bottom of all three layers taking a small seam allowance. Do this for both sides of the tea cosy.

8 Fold back the lining so that you are looking at two large oval shapes, half lining and half patterned.

9 Place the two sides of the cosy together, right sides facing and seams matching, and sew all the way round. Leave a gap in the lining side of around 4in (10cm) for turning.

10 Turn right sides out.

11 Topstitch across the gap, and then push the lining up into the tea cosy.

12 Press, then put the kettle on!

Sewing Machine Dust Cover

Many sewing machines come with a flimsy plastic dust cover. It's important to keep your machine dust-free, so why not replace it with a pretty handmade cover that you'll be proud to show off!

What you need

Two pieces of fabric each 16 x 12in (40.5 x 30.5cm), or measure the width and height of your sewing machine and add 1in (2.5cm) to each side

One piece of fabric 16in (40.5cm) wide (or the width of your sewing machine plus 1in [2.5cm]) x 6in (15cm) for the top

Two pieces of fabric each 12in (30.5cm) high (or the height of your sewing machine plus 1in [2.5cm]) x 7in (18cm) for the sides

Pieces of wadding cut to the same sizes as all of the above

One piece of fabric 6in (15cm) square for the pocket

Rectangle of fabric 8 x 4in (20.5 x 10cm) for the handle

1½yd (1.4m) of bias-binding tape

Four buttons

1 Measure the height of your sewing machine and its width at its widest point. Then measure the depth at both the top and bottom as most machines taper slightly. Mine measures 14in (35.5cm) wide, 10in (25.5cm) high, 6in (15cm) deep at the bottom and 5in (13cm) deep at the top. I've cut my fabric 1in (2.5cm) bigger than each of these measurements so that the cover isn't too snug.

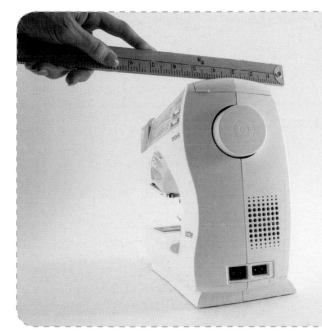

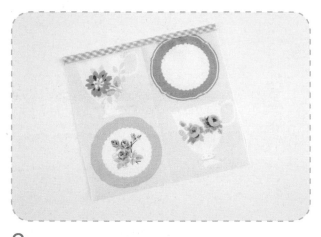

Tip
The same measuring method could be used for a serger, kitchen appliances or even your PC!

2 Sew a piece of bias binding across the top edge of the pocket (see page 14).

3 Fold the three remaining sides in by ¼in (0.5cm) and press the folds in place.

4 Find the centre point of the front of the cover by folding it in half and creasing. Pin the pocket to the centre and sew down the sides and along the bottom, back-tacking at the start and end of your stitches to secure. I've used the same fabric for the cover and for the pocket and so have matched the pattern on each. You may find it easier to use a contrasting or plain fabric for the pocket.

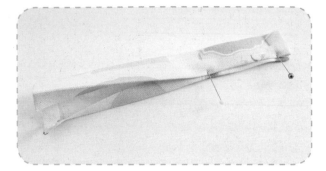

5 Next, make the handle. Fold under the short ends by ¼in (0.5cm) and press. Then fold the length in half and press again. Finally, open up the length and fold the raw edges into the centre, re-fold in half, pin and press again.

6 Measure the centre point of the top section of the cover. Pin the handle 2in (5cm) each side of this mark then sew it in place. Your handle should be arched, not completely flat. To hide the stitches, sew four buttons, one on top of the other, on each side.

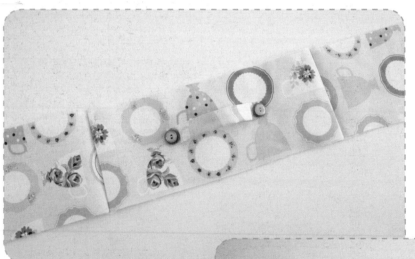

7 Using fabric adhesive spray, line each panel of fabric with wadding.

8 Join the two side panels to the top panel.

9 Next, centre the front panel on the top piece, right sides facing, then pin in place and sew the two together across the top taking a ¼in (0.5cm) seam allowance.

10 Starting from the top, stitch the sides together, taking a ¼in (0.5cm) seam allowance. You should see the box shape starting to take shape.

Tip

If your sewing machine has a top handle, you could make a long hole in the top of your cover to pull the handle through. Alternatively, a pretty ribbon could be used for a handle, or a plaited cord knotted at the ends.

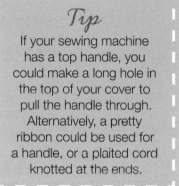

11 Attach the second side panel in the same way.

12 Snip across the corners of the seam allowances to remove excess fabric before turning the right way out.

13 Apply bias binding all the way round the bottom of the dust cover and press (see page 14).

String of Hearts

Add as many hearts as you like, change the colours and the embellishments used and you can make a pretty decoration that will enhance any room in the house, whatever your style. A trim of lace around the seam makes the hearts even more feminine. Try stringing together even more hearts in varying sizes, add another ribbon loop at the other end and create a swag or make a single heart into a pincushion (see page 11).

(see page 11)

What you need

Woven cotton fabric in two different designs, each piece around 12in (30.5cm) square

Four pieces of card to make templates

Wadding

Approximately 16in (5cm) of matching ribbon

Eight buttons to decorate

Four round lids ranging in size from about 2in (5cm) to about 4in (10cm) diameter

1 Fold the card in half. Place one of the lids just over the fold, and draw around the circle as shown.

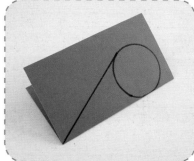

2 With a ruler, make a line from the edge of the circle to the fold. The shorter your line the fatter your heart will be!

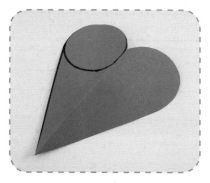

3 Cut out the shape and there's your heart template. Repeat using the other three lids.

4 Use your templates to cut two hearts in each size.

5 Place each pair of hearts right sides together and sew all the way round, starting at the side and leaving a gap of around 1½in (4cm) for turning the fabric through.

6 Cut little 'v' shapes out of the curved edges and snip across the tip of the heart. This will help to keep the seam neat when turning.

7 Turn each heart the right way out, then insert the wadding until the heart is quite firm and plump. Hand sew over the gap with a ladder stitch.

Tip
When stuffing, add a little dried lavender for a delightfully fragrant aroma.

8 Arrange the hearts with the largest at the top and the smallest at the bottom, then hand sew the point of the top one to the top of the next. Continue until all four hearts are joined together.

9 To decorate, sew two or three buttons at the top of each heart. At the top of the string of hearts, hand sew the ribbon in a loop and add a pretty bow to hide the stitches.

Tissue Box Cover

Use any pretty woven fabric to cover your tissue box for a delightfully coordinated, feminine look. For the man in your life, try using denim or linen for a more masculine look.

What you need

Approximately 12 x 12in (30.5 x 30.5cm) of cotton fabric, depending on the size of your tissue box

Approximately 24in (61cm) of bias-binding tape and the same length of ¼in (0.5cm) diameter piping cord

Ribbon for the ties

1 Measure the length, depth and width of your tissue box. Mark the centre line on each side of the box and note the measurements so that you don't forget them!

2 Cut one piece of fabric to this size, adding an extra ½in (1cm) to the width for the seam allowance.

3 Cover your piping cord in bias-binding tape, following the instructions on page 15. Pin the bias binding in place around the cord, put the zipper foot on to your sewing machine and sew along the bias binding quite close to the cord. Cut the length in half.

> *Tip*
> If you don't want to use piping, just finish off the opening with coordinating bias binding.

4 Apply the piping to the edges of the fabric that will form the opening at the top, following the instructions on page 15. Back-tack at each end of your sewing to secure the stitches.

5 Place the fabric face down on your worktop, fold it in half and finger crease the centre line.

6 Fold the two bound edges together, meeting on the creased line, and pin.

7 Sew the side seams taking a ¼in (0.5cm) seam allowance and sewing over the cord and binding ends a couple of times to reinforce the weakest point of the cover.

8 Keeping the cover inside out, insert your tissue box, lining up the opening in the cover with the central line you marked on the box.

9 Pinch the fabric at the corners, and put a dot on the top and bottom corners using a non-permanent fabric marker.

10 Remove the box from the sleeve. Flatten one corner and join the top and bottom dots with a drawn line. Do this on all four corners.

11 Sew along each drawn line, back-tacking at each end, and you'll start to see the box shape developing.

12 Cut away the excess fabric at each corner.

13 Turn the cover out the right way and insert your tissue box. Sew a couple of ribbons on by hand either side of the opening and tie them in pretty bows to finish.

Index